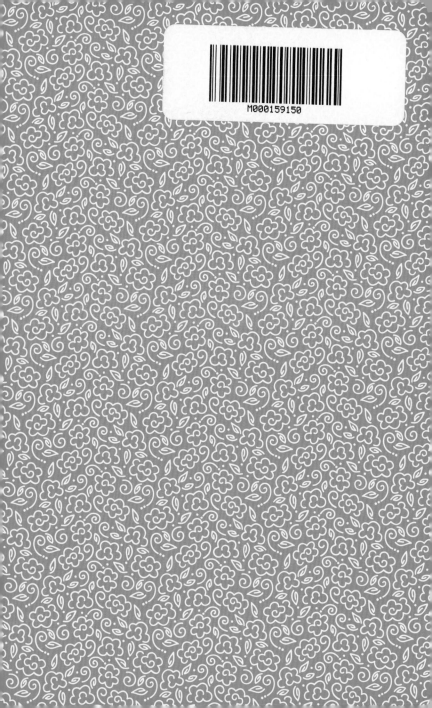

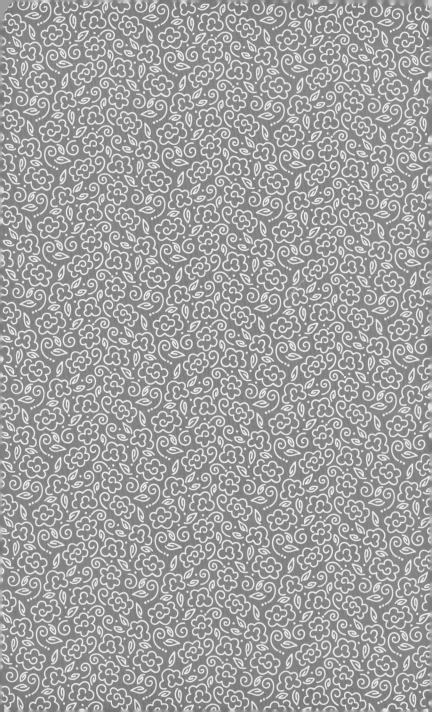

Presented to

_____

On the occasion of

_____

Published in Nashville, Tennessee, by Thomas Nelson.

Thomas Nelson titles may be purchased in bulk for educational, business, fund-raising, or sales promotional use. For information, please e-mail SpecialMarkets@ThomasNelson.com.

ISBN-13: 978-0-529-10557-8

Printed in China

14 15 16 17 18 TIMS 5 4 3 2 1

www.thomasnelson.com

Prayer Journal

STORMIE OMARTIAN

THOMAS NELSON
Since 1798

NASHVILLE   MEXICO CITY   RIO DE JANEIRO

You can't move into all God has for you if any doubt or lack of forgiveness has found a place in your heart.

Trust

 *Blessed are all those who
put their trust in Him.*

Psalm 2:12

Keep your life totally open before the Lord if you want to avoid the traps and consequences of sin.

_____
_____
_____
_____
_____
_____
_____
_____
_____
_____
_____
_____
_____
_____
_____
_____
_____
_____
_____

*Blessed is he whose
transgression is forgiven.*

Psalm 32:1

*P*rayer is talking with God. It's getting close to and spending time with the One you love.

Hope

I will love You, O LORD, my strength. . . . Your right hand has held me up, Your gentleness has made me great. You enlarged my path under me, so my feet did not slip.

PSALM 18:1, 35–36

*P*rayer is taking the time to say, "Speak to my heart, Lord, and tell me what I need to hear."

_____

_____

_____

_____

_____

_____

_____

_____

_____

_____

_____

_____

"Why do you spend money for what is not bread, and your wages for what does not satisfy? Listen carefully to Me, and eat what is good, and let your soul delight itself in abundance. Incline your ear, and come to Me. Hear, and your soul shall live."

ISAIAH 55:2–3

The more you pray, the more you will find to pray about, and the more you'll be led to pray for others.

_____
_____
_____
_____
_____
_____
_____
_____
_____
_____
_____
_____
_____
_____
_____
_____
_____

Trust

"So I say to you, ask, and it will
be given to you; seek, and you will
find; knock, and it will be opened to
you. For everyone who asks receives,
and he who seeks finds, and to him
who knocks it will be opened."

LUKE 11:9–10

$\mathcal{D}$on't allow discouragement over unanswered prayer to cause you to doubt that God has heard you. God hears you, and something is happening whether you see it manifested in your life now or not.

_____

_____

_____

_____

_____

_____

_____

_____

_____

_____

_____

_____

_____

*"My thoughts are not your thoughts,
nor are your ways My ways," says
the LORD. "For as the heavens are
higher than the earth, so are My
ways higher than your ways, and
My thoughts than your thoughts."*

ISAIAH 55:8–9

15

The word *sin* is an old archery term meaning "to miss the bull's-eye." Anything other than the center of God's best and perfect will for our lives is sin.

_____

_____

_____

_____

_____

_____

_____

_____

_____

_____

_____

_____

_____

_____

Hope

All have sinned and fall short
of the glory of God.

When sin is not confessed, it wraps its tentacles around every part of our being until we are paralyzed.

_____

_____

_____

_____

_____

_____

_____

_____

_____

_____

_____

_____

_____

_____

_____

_____

Whoever conceals their
sins does not prosper.

PROVERBS 28:13 NIV

> *We* don't have to be tortured by guilt. God provided the key to release us from that, and it is confession.

Love

If we confess our sins, He is faithful
and just to forgive us our sins and to
cleanse us from all unrighteousness.

When sin is left unconfessed, a wall goes up between you and God.

Trust

_____

_____

_____

_____

_____

_____

_____

_____

_____

_____

_____

_____

_____

_Your iniquities have separated you
from your God; and your sins have
hidden His face from you, so that
He will not hear. For your hands are
defiled with blood, and your fingers
with iniquity; your lips have spoken lies,
your tongue has muttered perversity._

Isaiah 59:2–3

*E*ven if we feel justified in having anger or bitterness toward someone, we must still confess it because it misses the mark of what God has for us. If we don't get free of that, the weight of it will eventually crush us.

 Let all bitterness, wrath, anger, clamor, and evil speaking be put away from you, with all malice.

EPHESIANS 4:31

Repentance literally means "a change of mind." It means to turn your back, walk away, and decide not to do it again.

_____

_____

_____

_____

_____

_____

_____

_____

_____

_____

_____

_____

_____

_____

_____

_____

Hope

*Incline my heart to Your testimonies,
and not to covetousness. Turn away
my eyes from looking at worthless
things, and revive me in Your way.*

PSALM 119:36–37

Confessing is speaking the whole truth about your sin. *Renouncing* is taking a firm stand against it and removing its right to stay.

Love

Blessed is he whose transgression
is forgiven, whose sin is covered.
Blessed is the man to whom the
LORD does not impute iniquity, and
in whose spirit there is no deceit.

PSALM 32:1–2

*W*hile you can't see all your errors all the time, you can have a heart that is willing to be taught by the Lord. Ask God to bring to light sins you are not aware of so they can be confessed, repented of, and forgiven.

Trust

 Who can discern their own errors?
Forgive my hidden faults.

PSALM 19:12 NIV

> *Always keep in mind that God's ways are for your benefit.*

 I know the thoughts that I think toward you, says the LORD, thoughts of peace and not of evil, to give you a future and a hope.

JEREMIAH 29:11

Confession is for you to be made whole. . . . People who confess find mercy and God's unlimited power.

*I acknowledged my sin to You, and my
iniquity I have not hidden. I said, "I will
confess my transgressions to the* LORD,*"
and You forgave the iniquity of my sin.*

PSALM 32:5

On the cross Jesus took all of my sin, brokenness, fear, sadness, rejection, and death and gave me His forgiveness, peace, joy, wholeness, acceptance, and life.

_____

_____

_____

_____

_____

_____

_____

_____

_____

_____

_____

_____

_____

_____

_____

_____

*"Most assuredly, I say to you, he who
hears My word and believes in Him
who sent Me has everlasting life, and
shall not come into judgment, but
has passed from death into life."*

JOHN 5:24

My two children have been the greatest examples of God's mercy and grace to me. *God gave me what I did not deserve.*

By the grace of God I am what I am.

1 CORINTHIANS 15:10 NIV

God's grace keeps us from suffering the consequences of our sin. God's mercy is His love and compassion manifested toward us. We need both.

Trust

But He was wounded for our
transgressions, He was bruised for our
iniquities; the chastisement for our
peace was upon Him, and by His stripes
we are healed. All we like sheep have
gone astray; we have turned, every
one, to his own way; and the LORD has
laid on Him the iniquity of us all.

ISAIAH 53:5–6

Although it's hard to comprehend love so great, I believe You laid down Your life for me so that I might have life eternally and abundantly now.

_____

_____

_____

_____

_____

_____

_____

_____

 *Being found in appearance as a man,
[Jesus] humbled Himself and became
obedient to the point of death, even
the death of the cross. Therefore God
also has highly exalted Him and given
Him the name which is above every
name, that at the name of Jesus every
knee should bow, of those in heaven,
and of those on earth, and of those
under the earth, and that every tongue
should confess that Jesus Christ is
Lord, to the glory of God the Father.*

PHILIPPIANS 2:8–11

When you acknowledge Jesus as Savior, He will guide you where you need to go.

In all your ways acknowledge Him,
and He shall direct your paths.

PROVERBS 3:6

The Holy Spirit is the Spirit of God
sent by Jesus to give us comfort, . . .
to guide us in all truth, . . . [and]
to help us pray more effectively.

_____

_____

_____

_____

_____

_____

_____

_____

_____

_____

_____

_____

_____

_____

_____

_____

_____

_____

_____

 "When He, the Spirit of truth, has come, He will guide you into all truth."

JOHN 16:13

I learned three important reasons to be filled with God's Spirit: to worship more fully; to experience and communicate God's love more completely; and to appropriate God's power in my life more effectively.

_____

_____

_____

_____

_____

_____

_____

_____

_____

_____

_____

_____

_____

Love

God has not given us a spirit
of fear, but of power and of
love and of a sound mind.

2 TIMOTHY 1:7

> The infilling of the Holy Spirit
> is ongoing and ever deepening.

_____

_____

_____

_____

_____

_____

_____

_____

_____

_____

_____

_____

_____

_____

_____

_____

Trust

John answered, saying to all, "I indeed baptize you with water; but One mightier than I is coming, whose sandal strap I am not worthy to loose. He will baptize you with the Holy Spirit and fire."

LUKE 3:16

You don't have to feel like forgiving someone. Forgiveness is something you do out of obedience to the Lord because He has forgiven *you*.

"If your brother sins against you,
rebuke him; and if he repents, forgive
him. And if he sins against you seven
times in a day, and seven times
in a day returns to you, saying, 'I
repent,' you shall forgive him."

LUKE 17:3–4

> *Forgiveness leads to life.*
> *Unforgiveness is a slow death.*

When I kept silent, my bones grew old through my groaning all the day long. For day and night Your hand was heavy upon me; my vitality was turned into the drought of summer.

Psalm 32:3–4

Forgiveness has to do with remembering that God is the only One who knows the whole story; therefore, we never have the right to judge another person.

_____

_____

_____

_____

_____

_____

_____

_____

_____

_____

_____

_____

_____

_____

Trust

 God is a just judge.

PSALM 7:11

*U*nless we truly let Jesus penetrate every part of our lives, we won't ever really know what God is like.

_____

_____

_____

_____

_____

_____

_____

_____

_____

_____

_____

_____

_____

_____

_____

_____

 "He who has seen Me has seen the Father."

JOHN 14:9

When you truly know Jesus, you see that Father God is faithful and compassionate. His love is unlimited and unfailing.

Hope

Because of the LORD's great love we
are not consumed, for his compassions
never fail. They are new every
morning; great is your faithfulness.

LAMENTATIONS 3:22–23 NIV

> *Lord,* take away my misconceptions about You and help me know You better.

_____

_____

_____

_____

_____

_____

_____

_____

_____

_____

_____

_____

_____

_____

_____

 You are God, ready to pardon, gracious and merciful, slow to anger, abundant in kindness.

NEHEMIAH 9:17

*B*e honest with God if you are angry with Him. Release the hurt to Him and let yourself cry. Tears are freeing and healing.

_____
_____
_____
_____
_____
_____
_____
_____
_____
_____
_____
_____
_____
_____

Love

Put my tears into Your bottle.

PSALM 56:8

People tend to view God the same way they viewed their parents. It takes a time of healing, deliverance, and getting to know the unconditional love of God before total trust comes.

_____

_____

_____

_____

_____

_____

_____

_____

_____

_____

 "If a son asks for bread from any father among you, will he give him a stone? Or if he asks for a fish, will he give him a serpent instead of a fish? Or if he asks for an egg, will he offer him a scorpion? If you then, being evil, know how to give good gifts to your children, how much more will your heavenly Father give the Holy Spirit to those who ask Him!"

LUKE 11:11–13

> *Bitterly painful experiences will continue to hurt you if you don't cry out your pain to the Lord.*

_____

_____

_____

_____

_____

_____

_____

_____

_____

_____

_____

_____

_____

_____

_____

_____

_____

_____

_____

_____

_____

_____

_____

_____

_____

_____

_____

_____

_____

_____

_____

*In my distress I called upon the LORD,
and cried out to my God; He heard
my voice from His temple, and my cry
came before Him, even to His ears.*

PSALM 18:6

In times of weakness, when life seems out of control, choose to put yourself under God's control.

_____

_____

_____

_____

_____

_____

_____

_____

Hope

_____

_____

He gives power to the weak, and to those who have no might He increases strength. Even the youths shall faint and be weary, and the young men shall utterly fall, but those who wait on the LORD shall renew their strength; they shall mount up with wings like eagles, they shall run and not be weary, they shall walk and not faint.

ISAIAH 40:29–31

God is a God of restoration and redemption, so He can redeem whatever has occurred in your past.

The Spirit of the Lord GOD is upon Me . . . He has sent Me to heal the brokenhearted . . . to comfort all who mourn . . . to give them beauty for ashes, the oil of joy for mourning.

Why do we refuse to obey God when He asks us to forgive others as He has forgiven us? It's because we focus on the person who has wronged us rather than on God who makes all things right.

Love

"Therefore I say to you, her sins, which are many, are forgiven, for she loved much. But to whom little is forgiven, the same loves little."

LUKE 7:47

Forgiveness doesn't make
the other person right;
forgiveness makes you free.

_____

_____

_____

_____

_____

_____

_____

_____

_____

_____

_____

_____

_____

_____

_____

 Then Jesus said to those Jews who believed Him, "If you abide in My word, you are My disciples indeed. And you shall know the truth, and the truth shall make you free."

JOHN 8:31–32

The best way to turn anger, bitterness, hatred, and resentment for someone into love is to pray for that person. God softens your heart when you do.

Hope

 *"You shall love your
neighbor as yourself."*

MATTHEW 22:39

*J*esus wants me to acknowledge Him as Lord over *every* area of my life.

"Why do you call Me 'Lord, Lord,'
and not do the things which I say?"

Jesus will never bulldoze His way in and break down the walls of your heart. He will simply knock persistently and quietly, and as He's invited, will come to gently occupy each corner to clean, renew, and rebuild.

Trust

"Behold, I stand at the door and knock.
If anyone hears My voice and opens
the door, I will come in to him and
dine with him, and he with Me."

REVELATION 3:20

*W*ill you choose to open up and
share every part of yourself with Jesus
and let Him reign in your life?

O Lord, You have searched me and
known me. You know my sitting down
and my rising up; You understand
my thought afar off. You comprehend
my path and my lying down, and are
acquainted with all my ways. For there
is not a word on my tongue, but behold,
O Lord, You know it altogether.

Psalm 139:1–4

*T*rue rest is being still and knowing that God is God—no matter what is happening around us.

Be still, and know that I am God.

PSALM 46:10

> *Resting is being able to say, "God is in charge, I have prayed about it, He knows my need, and I can rest in Him."*

Love

The LORD reigns; let the earth
rejoice. . . . Righteousness and justice
are the foundation of His throne.

PSALM 97:1–2

A time comes when each of us must place our desires and dreams in the hands of God so that He can free us from those that are not in His will.

Trust

"Our God whom we serve is able
to deliver us from the burning fiery
furnace, and He will deliver us from
your hand, O king. But if not, let it be
known to you, O king, that we do not
serve your gods, nor will we worship the
gold image which you have set up."

How many times do we ask God to give us what we want, but we don't give God what He wants?

_____

_____

_____

_____

_____

_____

_____

_____

_____

_____

_____

_____

_____

_____

_____

I acknowledge my transgressions,
and my sin is always before me.
Against You, You only, have I sinned,
and done this evil in Your sight.

PSALM 51:3–4

God has set up certain rules to protect us and to work for our benefit. He designed us and knows what will fulfill us most.

Hope

I will instruct you and teach you in the way you should go; I will guide you with My eye.

PSALM 32:8

Anyone who hears the words of the Lord and does not put them into practice is like someone who builds a house with no foundation. When the storm comes, it will collapse and be destroyed.

"Everyone who hears these sayings of Mine, and does not do them, will be like a foolish man who built his house on the sand: and the rain descended, the floods came, and the winds blew and beat on that house; and it fell. And great was its fall."

MATTHEW 7:26–27

We cannot feel or enjoy God's love for us if we're not living as He intended us to live, in total submission to His Word and His will.

Love

 *Your word is a lamp to my feet
and a light to my path.*

PSALM 119:105

When we praise the Lord, the prison doors of our lives are opened, our bonds are broken, and we are set free. Praising God opens our hearts to better experience His love.

Trust

Praise the LORD! Praise God in His sanctuary; praise Him in His mighty firmament! Praise Him for His mighty acts; praise Him according to His excellent greatness! . . . Let everything that has breath praise the LORD.

PSALM 150:1–2, 6

Now is the time to lift up a prayer of praise to God for everything in your life. Start with thanking Him for His Word, His faithfulness, His love, His grace, His healing, and continue on from there.

Hope

Every good gift and every perfect gift is from above.

JAMES 1:17

*I*n the Old Testament, the people who carried the ark of the covenant stopped every six steps to worship. We also have to remind ourselves not to go very far without stopping to praise and worship. We each must learn to be a six-step person. Enter into His gates with thanksgiving, and into His courts with praise. Be thankful to Him, and bless His name.

_____
_____
_____
_____
_____
_____
_____
_____
_____
_____
_____
_____
_____
_____
_____
_____
_____
_____

*For the LORD is good; His mercy
is everlasting, and His truth
endures to all generations.*

PSALM 100:5

With praise, you and your circumstances can be changed, because praise gives God entrance into your life and allows Him to be enthroned there.

Love

Let us continually offer the sacrifice of praise to God, that is, the fruit of our lips, giving thanks to His name.

HEBREWS 13:15

Thank God that in any weak area of your life, He will be strong. Thank Him that He came to restore you. Remember the names of the Lord, and use them in prayer. "I praise You, Lord, because You are my Deliverer and Redeemer." "Thank You, God, that You are my Healer and Provider."

Trust

"My grace is sufficient for you, for My strength is made perfect in weakness."

2 CORINTHIANS 12:9

We can overcome a critical attitude by being constantly filled with the love of the Lord through worship, praise, and thanksgiving toward Him.

_____

_____

_____

_____

_____

_____

_____

_____

_____

_____

_____

_____

_____

_____

_____

_____

_____

_____

_____

_____

 *O Lord, our Lord, how excellent is
Your name in all the earth, who have
set Your glory above the heavens!*

PSALM 8:1

Praise is your greatest weapon against fear, so use it. That's because your praise invites God's presence, and in His presence there is no reason to fear.

Hope

"Fear not, for I am with you; be
not dismayed, for I am your God.
I will strengthen you, yes, I will
help you, I will uphold you with
My righteous right hand."

ISAIAH 41:10

The best way to focus on God is to thank Him continually for all He has given, praise Him for all He has done, and worship Him for all that He is. It's impossible to be self-absorbed while you are glorifying and praising God!

Love

Rejoice always, pray continually, give thanks in all circumstances; for this is God's will for you in Christ Jesus.

1 THESSALONIANS 5:16–18 NIV

> *In* times of unanswered prayer, waiting produces patience. When you are patient, you are able to place yourself in God's hands.

Trust

*Let us run with endurance the race
that is set before us, looking unto Jesus,
the author and finisher of our faith.*

HEBREWS 12:1–2

God is in control whether it is a bright day or a dark night in your soul.

In all these things we are more than conquerors through Him who loved us.

ROMANS 8:37

The prayer of praise is a way of reminding ourselves that God hears our every prayer. Even when we feel like nothing is going on in God's kingdom, His love, healing, and redemption are always going on.

_____

_____

_____

_____

_____

_____

_____

_____

_____

_____

_____

_____

_____

_____

_____

_____

_____

 Our light affliction, which is but for a moment, is working for us a far more exceeding and eternal weight of glory.

2 CORINTHIANS 4:17

> *No life is an accident or is unwanted in God's eyes.*

_____

_____

_____

_____

_____

_____

_____

_____

_____

_____

_____

_____

_____

_____

_____

_____

_____

You created my inmost being; you knit me together in my mother's womb. I praise you because I am fearfully and wonderfully made.

Psalm 139:13–14 NIV

*A*llow God to show you what He thinks of you and let it sink in and penetrate every fiber of your being.

Trust

> *Behold what manner of love the Father has bestowed on us, that we should be called children of God!*
>
> 1 JOHN 3:1

Learn to value yourself as God values you by deliberately thanking and praising Him for any positive things you see. Say, "Thank You, Lord, that I can breathe, that I can talk, that I can see, that I know You." Praise God for specific things, for that is the best medicine to help you stop believing lies about yourself.

_The LORD your God in your midst,
the Mighty One, will save; He will
rejoice over you with gladness, He
will quiet you with His love, He will
rejoice over you with singing._

ZEPHANIAH 3:17

When the devil tries to tear you down with lies about yourself, praise God for who He made you to be.

Hope

_By this we know love, because
He laid down His life for us._

When you understand that God has a plan for your life and that as long as you walk in His will, your future is secure in His hands, you will never want to be without Jesus and all He has for you.

Faith

"Peace I leave with you, My peace I give to you; not as the world gives do I give to you. Let not your heart be troubled, neither let it be afraid."

JOHN 14:27

> *P*raying God's Word enlarges your faith and encourages you to believe for the answers to your prayers.

Trust

Through the LORD's mercies we are not
consumed, because His compassions
fail not. They are new every morning;
great is Your faithfulness.

LAMENTATIONS 3:22–23

> *Praying God's promises helps you pray in line with God's will.*

"Abba, Father, all things are possible for You. Take this cup away from Me; nevertheless, not what I will, but what You will."

MARK 14:36

When I realized that God looks at us in light of the future He has for us, I was able to stop judging myself because of my past.

Hope

I press on, that I may lay hold of that for which Christ Jesus has also laid hold of me. Brethren, I do not count myself to have apprehended; but one thing I do, forgetting those things which are behind and reaching forward to those things which are ahead, I press toward the goal for the prize of the upward call of God in Christ Jesus.

PHILIPPIANS 3:12–14

God looks at us the way He made us to be. Although He accepts us just as we are, He isn't going to leave us that way. Because He loves us so much, He is going to enable us to become all He created us to be.

The fruit of the Spirit is love, joy, peace,
longsuffering, kindness, goodness,
faithfulness, gentleness, self-control.
Against such there is no law.

GALATIANS 5:22–23

God doesn't expect us to be perfect in *performance*, but perfect in *heart*. We need to know that God *already* views us as perfect when He looks in our hearts and sees Jesus there.

Trust

"The LORD does not see as man sees; for
man looks at the outward appearance,
but the LORD looks at the heart."

1 SAMUEL 16:7

When you pray, thank God for the good things He says about you. It will help you believe them!

 "Since you [are] precious in My sight, you have been honored, and I have loved you."

ISAIAH 43:4

God is a good God.

 Good and upright is the LORD.

PSALM 25:8

God is on my side.

Love

_The LORD is on my side; I will not
fear. What can man do to me?_

PSALM 118:6

God's laws and ways
are for my benefit.

Trust

_By [Your law and commandments]
Your servant is warned, and in
keeping them there is great reward._

God is always with me.

_____

_____

_____

_____

_____

_____

_____

_____

_____

_____

_____

_____

_____

_____

_____

_____

_____

_____

_____

_____

_____

_____

_____

_____

_____

_____

_____

_____

_____

_____

_____

I am persuaded that neither death nor life, nor angels nor principalities nor powers, nor things present nor things to come, nor height nor depth, nor any other created thing, shall be able to separate us from the love of God which is in Christ Jesus our Lord.

ROMANS 8:38–39

God wants me restored.

_____

_____

_____

_____

_____

_____

_____

_____

_____

_____

_____

_____

_____

_____

_____

_____

_____

_____

Hope

If anyone is in Christ, he is a new
creation; old things have passed away;
behold, all things have become new.

2 CORINTHIANS 5:17

God's promises to me will never fail.

 Your faithfulness endures to all generations; You established the earth, and it abides.

PSALM 119:90

We may think we must give serious credence to everything that comes into our minds, but we don't. We only have to examine our thoughts in the light of the Word of God and see if they line up properly.

Love

Examine me, O LORD, and prove
me; try my mind and my heart.

PSALM 26:2

All evil happens by deception. The enemy entices us to accept things that are in opposition to God's ways.

The serpent said to the woman, "You will not surely die. For God knows that in the day you eat of it your eyes will be opened, and you will be like God, knowing good and evil."

GENESIS 3:4–5

You are either lined up with God's kingdom or with Satan's. We make that choice every day.

_____

_____

_____

_____

_____

_____

_____

_____

_____

_____

_____

_____

_____

*The law of the Lord is perfect, refreshing
the soul. The statutes of the Lord are
trustworthy, making wise the simple.
The precepts of the Lord are right, giving
joy to the heart. The commands of the
Lord are radiant, giving light to the eyes.*

PSALM 19:7–8 NIV

Without God's Word filling your mind with truth, you can't identify the enemy's lies. And without daily praying, "Lord, keep me undeceived," you can't ward off the deceiver.

Hope

The word of God is living and powerful,
and sharper than any two-edged
sword, piercing even to the division
of soul and spirit, and of joints and
marrow, and is a discerner of the
thoughts and intents of the heart.

HEBREWS 4:12

Everything you don't know about God will be used against you by the enemy.

_____

_____

_____

_____

_____

_____

_____

_____

_____

_____

_____

_____

*All Scripture is given by inspiration of
God, and is profitable for doctrine, for
reproof, for correction, for instruction
in righteousness, that the man of
God may be complete, thoroughly
equipped for every good work.*

2 TIMOTHY 3:16–17

One reason we do not have the wholeness, fulfillment, and peace we desire is that we have not acknowledged God as the answer to our every need.

_____

_____

_____

_____

_____

_____

_____

_____

_____

_____

_____

_____

_____

_____

_____

Love

"Do not worry, saying, 'What shall we eat?' or 'What shall we drink?' or 'What shall we wear?' For after all these things the Gentiles seek. For your heavenly Father knows that you need all these things. But seek first the kingdom of God and His righteousness, and all these things shall be added to you."

MATTHEW 6:31–33

Lord, You are my Counselor.

_____

_____

_____

_____

_____

_____

_____

_____

_____

_____

_____

_____

_____

_____

_____

_____

_____

Trust

For unto us a Child is born, unto us a
Son is given; and the government will be
upon His shoulder. And His name will
be called Wonderful, Counselor, Mighty
God, Everlasting Father, Prince of Peace.

ISAIAH 9:6

Lord, You are my Deliverer.

_____

_____

_____

_____

_____

_____

_____

_____

_____

_____

_____

_____

_____

_____

_____

_____

_____

*The LORD is my rock and my fortress
and my deliverer; my God, my strength,
in whom I will trust; my shield and the
horn of my salvation, my stronghold.*

Jesus, thank You that You are *Emmanuel*, "God with us."

Hope

"Lo, I am with you always,
even to the end of the age."

MATTHEW 28:20

Lord, You are my Friend.

_____

_____

_____

_____

_____

_____

_____

_____

_____

_____

_____

_____

_____

_____

 *"No longer do I call you servants, for a
servant does not know what his master
is doing; but I have called you friends,
for all things that I heard from My
Father I have made known to you."*

Lord, You are my Restorer.

Love

He restores my soul; He leads
me in the paths of righteousness
for His name's sake.

PSALM 23:3

177

Lord, You are my Comforter.

Trust

Blessed be the God and Father of our
Lord Jesus Christ, the Father of mercies
and God of all comfort, who comforts
us in all our tribulation, that we may
be able to comfort those who are in any
trouble, with the comfort with which
we ourselves are comforted by God.

2 CORINTHIANS 1:3–4

 *Behold, God is my salvation, I will trust and not be afraid; "For Y*AH*, the* L*ORD*, is my strength and song; He also has become my salvation."*

Lord, You are my Hope.

Hope

For You are my hope, O Lord GOD;
You are my trust from my youth.

PSALM 71:5

Lord, You are my Resting Place.

_____

_____

_____

_____

_____

_____

_____

_____

_____

_____

_____

_____

_____

_____

_____

"Come to Me, all you who labor and are heavy laden, and I will give you rest. Take My yoke upon you and learn from Me, for I am gentle and lowly in heart, and you will find rest for your souls."

MATTHEW 11:28–29

Lord, You are my Fortress.

_____

_____

_____

_____

_____

_____

_____

_____

_____

_____

_____

_____

_____

_____

_____

_____

_____

Love

The Lᴏʀᴅ is my rock and my fortress
and my deliverer; my God, my strength,
in whom I will trust; my shield and the
horn of my salvation, my stronghold.

Pꜱᴀʟᴍ 18:2

_____

_____

_____

_____

_____

_____

_____

_____

_____

_____

_____

_____

_____

_____

_____

_____

_____

Trust

You have been a strength to the poor, a strength to the needy in his distress, a refuge from the storm, a shade from the heat.

<small>ISAIAH 25:4</small>

> *God* is powerful on our behalf and loves us to the fullest possible measure.

"For God so loved the world that
He gave His only begotten Son, that
whoever believes in Him should not
perish but have everlasting life."

JOHN 3:16

If you feel powerless and weak in the face of your circumstances, then thank God that even though *you* are weak, *He* is not.

[Jesus] said to [me], "My grace is sufficient for you, for My strength is made perfect in weakness." Therefore most gladly I will rather boast in my infirmities, that the power of Christ may rest upon me.

2 CORINTHIANS 12:9

> *Faith is a spiritual muscle that needs to be exercised.*

 We walk by faith, not by sight.

2 CORINTHIANS 5:7

Every time we decide to trust the Lord for anything, we build our faith.

Love

Let the morning bring me word of your unfailing love, for I have put my trust in you. Show me the way I should go, for to you I entrust my life.

PSALM 143:8 NIV

*W*hat you speak promotes either
health and life, or sickness and death.

Trust

*A wholesome tongue
is a tree of life.*

PROVERBS 15:4

Faith is a gift from God because He enables us to believe, but we have to obey by building on that faith.

For by grace you have been saved
through faith, and that not of
yourselves; it is the gift of God, not
of works, lest anyone should boast.

 EPHESIANS 2:8–9

> *Reading the Word daily,
> listening to sound Bible teaching,
> and speaking the Word aloud
> will build your trust in God.*

Hope

"Man shall not live by bread alone,
but by every word that proceeds
from the mouth of God."

When talking about yourself, speak words of hope, health, encouragement, life, and purpose—they are God's truth for you.

Let the words of my mouth and the meditation of my heart be acceptable in Your sight, O LORD, my strength and my Redeemer.

> *Faith is our daily decision to trust God.*

Love

*Trust in the L*ORD* with all your heart, and lean not on your own understanding.*

PROVERBS 3:5

Prayer Requests and Answers

Prayer Requests and Answers

Prayer Requests and Answers

Prayer Requests and Answers

Prayer Requests and Answers

Prayer Requests and Answers

Prayer Requests and Answers

Prayer Requests and Answers

Prayer Requests and Answers

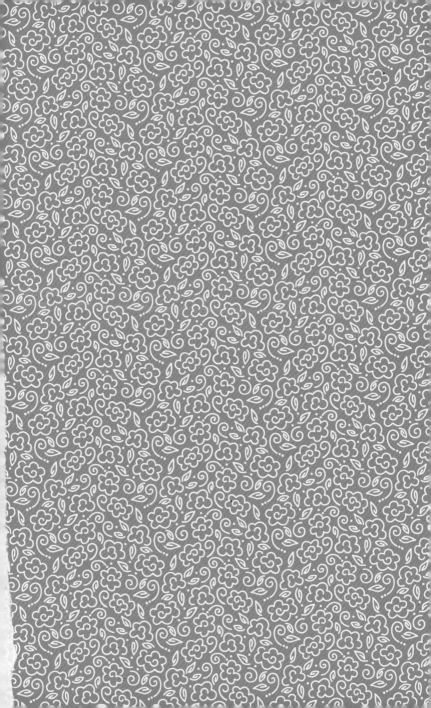

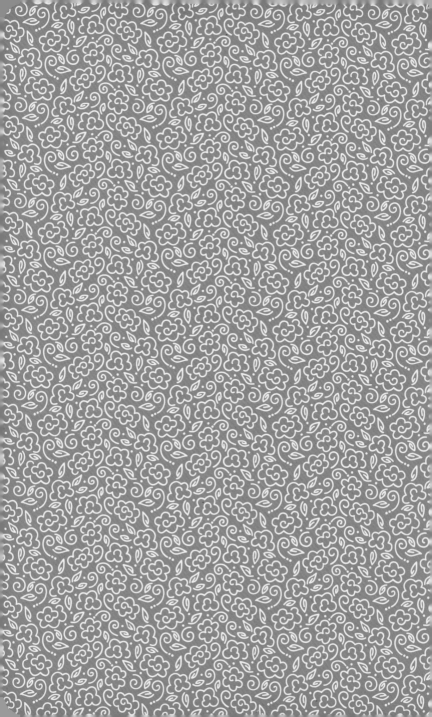